MW01601759

Poems for the Lost

by Joanie Terrizzi

The following pages contain poems written in the middle of 2021 for the lost among and within all of us. For more poems and information visit https://www.facebook.com/drjtpoetry

© 2021 Joanie Terrizzi

Welcoming what is on its way in
and ushering what is on its way out.

Like with waves lapping at the shore:
which drops of water slap upon the sand
are none of my business.

Like with breath:
which molecules of air fill my lungs
are none of my business.

I am just here
breathing.

I sat next to a dear friend on Zoom.
She was deep sad,
"I'm here," I said.
"I'm grateful that you trust me
with your story
and your sadness.
I am honored to sit with you
and care about you
exactly as you are
right now."

Tears brimmed her eyes
as she asked,
"How am I supposed to help others,
if I am this broken, myself
If it's all so dark?"

"I think it keeps us humble,"
I said, as I felt
around the cracks
in my own heart.
"I think when we are able to
stay with our own pain without
running away, we are able to
sit with others in theirs."

She nodded as I reached into my own
well of sorrows, felt the depth
of pains I've felt.
Feeling what she might feel.
"I don't think we grief tenders

get away without feeling it ourselves.
I think it's how we meet
each other in it," I said,
across the miles and
meeting her in the center of it.

A green thumb
is not actually the thumb.
It is the ears;
it is a way of listening
to the plants.

No;
it is in the body -
it is a way of listening
with the whole body.
It is an ability to
get out of the way
and hear what the plants need,
what life needs.
To hear it with the body.

Hands in the dirt,
quietly coaxing vibrancy forth,
it is not lost on me
that the plants - and I -
start and end with dirt,
with the chance to glimmer
in between.

"…like two rivers running parallel,"
she said, flowing her hands
like streams in the air,
"they may never meet,
but they flow in the same direction."

And I remembered the sound
of rushing water,
the current in my veins
and in my bones.

I know what it's like
to flow like that,
to hear the sound of water
tumbling in the same direction;
water that I may never see,
a stream that may not cross
with mine.

But I know that river.
I know the mountain snow
from which it melted,
I know the gulf
that will swallow
all we have left to give.

I know that river
like I know my own name.

They say,
"But aren't things going
back to normal?"
As if there is a "normal"
to go back to.
As if my life has ever been
a predictable shape.
As if I have any control over this,
anyway.

There is nothing to
return to,
no rhythmic comfort
to soothe my woes,
no "at least this"
to fall back into.

My life - and I -
are not the shapes we once were,
nor could we ever pretend to be,
just to fit, for a moment.
Altered as we are,
we move in the only direction
we ever could:
forward.

Ever forward,
one foot lifted in complete unknown,
as always, unable to see the ground.
Dwelling in the corner of my being
that somehow still finds the belief

that my foot will land
exactly where it needs to.
That the ground I cannot see
is there.

My friend told me how she heard a man
extol the wondrous heart of his loving father.
"Never has there been a father
as wonderful as mine," he glowed,
"I was so deeply loved and cared for."

And she hated him,
as she wrestled with the wounds
her own father left her wrestling with.

Until one day –
the man shared a story
of the ache and pain and horror
wrought by his father.
"Why did you lie?" my friend asked.

"I didn't lie," the man replied,
"I told the truth I deserved;
I told the tale that made me who I am.
I told the story I could live with."

And right there over dinner with my friend,
I started to tell myself the truth I deserved,
the tale that can make me who I want to be:
"You wouldn't believe how much I have been loved,"
I whispered in my mind,
"I have been blessed with
so.
much.
love.
Unfathomable, undeniable,
incomparable, unconditional love."

I started to tell myself
a story I can live with.

We are here for each other's
freedom.

What if the only reason
you have never taken flight
is that no one has yet held mirrors
in just the right way to show you
the wings on your own back?

And what if, upon seeing your wings
you would know at your core
–immediately–
how to take to the skies,
and up you would soar
on your own strength?

What perspective would the skies offer?
How much awe would you feel?
And what would be possible after that?

What wonder:
that you could see yourself
through my eyes.
What wonder:
that I could see myself
through your eyes.

For we are the seers
of each other's wings.

Belonging nowhere in this vast world,
at dusk, I came upon three
old-growth trees
wrapped in ivy
glimmering with hundreds
upon hundreds
of fireflies –
twinkling glitter in the inky dark.

My breath caught in awe.

I decided to belong there,
amidst that which sparkles in the dark.

And I let that be enough.

Sometimes my life feels like
a dot-to-dot drawing, carefully removed
from a child's coloring book.
Connecting lines and numbers
strangely absent;
each dot its own
unstrung
punctuation.

"Where are the numbers?"
I ask,
"In what order do I connect these dots?
Which should be next to which?"
And there is no answer.
So I take one breath.
And then another.

And I look up to the stars
as if the answer would be
written in the sky.
And I remember generations upon generations
upon generations
of humans who found
shapes, pictures, meaning, direction
in the stars, in the sky.

And I want these dots to
make sense to me, to
show me where to go.
But I know it is my breath,
my being, that links my dots:

that *I* need to make sense to the dots,
that I need to show *them* where to go,
that it is my very breath
that holds this constellation together.

And even so,
I yearn for the threads
that weave a life together.
The tapestry that tells a story.
The blossoms to belong to,
an understanding of my place
in the flock of all breathing beings.

But perhaps I am flockless.
Adrift between shores,
belonging more to what will be
than to what has been.

And there are no threads for that -
no words for stories yet-to-unfold,
No map, no way of weaving.
No blossoms to show to others.

There is just this watching the sky,
and all its various slants of light.
And letting that be enough.

And sometimes in the dark
a firefly lights your way;

and then another,

and then another.

Maybe the point is not
to be able to see
where you are going.

Maybe the point is
to learn from that which
lights up the darkness
with its entire being.

The things that float away -
like balloons whose strings
slipped through grasping fingers,
trailing upward, afloat on
awe and horror – those things,
catching on the wind:
let them.

Let them, and you can watch
as all the things
that are not meant for you
float away.

Whether the sky is filled
with all that will not stay,
or whether one glittering,
deeply mattering thing
insists on floating onward:
let it, let them.

Let them, and watch, gaping.
Feel the open-faced
horror and awe
of the things that float away,
because it's all you can do, anyway.

You are not alone in this:
being so human in the face of
all that is truly beyond your control
as to be filled with the fullness
of the awe and horror of
the things that float away.

For every single
second that the
fog of pain lifts –
for every fraction
of a second –
I want to kneel
and kiss the ground.

These days,
with my face already
pressed to the ground
it is much easier
to kiss.

Not an ounce of gratitude
is lost on me.

What if the lost place
is not an accident?

What if that completely
unmoored sensation
is a gift from the part of you
that is more alive than
the dock that set you free?

"But I can't stand up
with these sea-legs!"
you proclaim.

But you do not need your legs
at all, to let go to the
rocking rhythm of the water.

So set your sea-legs down,
rest your weary bones,
let the sky accompany
(and perhaps delight) you.

Legs or no, the current will
take you where you need to be.

Night spills on the mountain,
dripping down on the trees,
the slope kissing the sky
under the cloak of darkness.
All I see is ink, and yet:

the fireflies
and the twinkling stars
and the shooting stars
are indistinguishable,
inextinguishable
points of light.

They remind me that –
near or far –
any amount of light
punctuates the dark.

Maybe even
the flicker in my heart
can do that.

When there are no arms to hold you,
let the mountains hold you,
let their ranges gather you in,
let them embrace you with their forests,
lay your burdens in their valleys.

Let the mountains figure it out,
let their wisdom guide your way;
the mountains have seen more
than human eyes or minds
could possibly envision.

And they already know your way
home.

Sometimes it is not a
fork in the road,
rather,
it is single road
that your feet find familiar
that walks you right up to
a swiftly flowing river.

The choice is not between
this way or that.
The river has her course
and her current beckons you forth.

The choice is:
are you going
downstream on the raft,
or are you going
downstream in the water?

I would choose the raft
every. single. time.
The river knows where she is going,
and I'd rather watch the birds cross the sky
than be dragged through the churn and swirl
as life pulls me
where I need to go.

I don't think
I have ever felt
as alive as I do
in this exact moment.

What a moment.

Tumbling down the river
with all the other moments.

We have read
the directions
to our hearts
upside down.
And so: we live
upside down.

When life sets us
on our feet
we feel disoriented, and
have to learn to live
with an upside up heart.

What a
twirling tumble
in our rib cage.

The one who is
at home in the darkness
allows night to fall
around their shoulders.

You wouldn't want
to lose sight of that one,
so you might lay
a wreath of stars
around their neck.

But that would only be
to find your own way home.
Those who've found
their way in the dark
don't need others' light to see.

But it helps us
find our way
together.

I'm imagining there
actually is a thread
leading me forward.

Gossamer,
completely unseen to
the untrained eye.

I keep asking:
What is holding up
the other end?

Content to never
know the answer.

You might have
convinced yourself
that the Unknown
had lurked far away.

The Unknown is never
further from you
than your own
beating heart.
In fact, it has
never guaranteed you
a single
heartbeat.

The same Unknown
that ravages your life
(periodically)
is the one that holds
all the mystery
and wondrous turns
in your story.

It is the same Unknown
that holds within it
the shape your life would take
if you let yourself know
(and live with)
your full capacity.

It has been hard work
removing boulders from
this river all my life
even as more came
crashing in, at times.

Oh, but this river –
do you see how it flows?
Can you imagine it
completely unhindered?

Regardless of how many
rocks are left
(I see them clearly)
this is the vision I hold
as I remove this rock
with my bare hands.

And I watch, my own eyes
the only two that know
the sweetness
of how much more freely
this little bit flows.

You cannot know
what you don't yet know,
ever.

You cannot see
what you've not yet seen.

For once you've seen it,
you've seen it.
And once you know it,
you know it.

It is no longer Beyond.

But between here and Beyond
there is *always* a leap.

And that leap
always traverses
some flavor of
Wild Unknown.

An experiment:

Think of
all the things
in the world
that are growing
in ways
you cannot see.

And know that

you

are one of them.

"There is no ground
underneath me!"
you scream.

But there has never been
ground underneath you.

Only the illusion of it.

You have been
practicing groundlessness
all your life

without even knowing it.

All of life exists
because of seeds.

Not only that string
of aliveness that weaves
through living things
to arrive on our plates
and nourish us.

But also, the aliveness
that is a result of
the reminder that
that which cracks open
in the darkness time
after time after time
is not a painful ending,
but is the beginning

of something tender
and true in us that
can no longer not emerge.

Just because the stars
create a picture does not
make them a constellation.

Just because the shoe fits
doesn't mean it's yours.

You can quack like a duck,
and not be a duck.

You can hold in your hands
a pile of evidence that looks
exactly like it supports
the opposite of what actually is.

The mind weaves stories
made out of words
that we already know.

Set the stories down
in order to make room
for the shape you are now.

Stop looking at the future.

You have no idea how many
miracles [both hard and soft]
stand between you and the
you that you will become.

Is your life even remotely
the shape you thought
it would be right now?

Your mind cannot fathom the
amount of light that can
slip through the fissures
your life has wrought.

You have nothing more to
fathom than the air
in your lungs
right now.

Set the burden down.

Heavy as it is,
it is not the anchor
you have been
searching for.

Your weightlessness can
allow you to float
on the whirling Unknown,
which will carry you
to where you need to go
weighed down, or no.

And oh! To arrive
(again and again)
with ever more of
your lightness intact.

Rather than avoiding the
unavoidable, let go into it.

Let it wrap you in its arms,
whatever flavor of storm
it may be.

You can feel the thunder
in your bones already,
and in avoiding it
you avoid the very
trembling marrow of yourself.

Rather than sleepwalking,
be right *here*
with the storm of the
unavoidable in your sinews

and with your whole aliveness.

And sometimes, one more drop
of Unknown-ness overflows you.

And as you spill over the sides
of yourself you can do nothing
but laugh with actual glee.

You have no idea where you're flowing,
and suddenly that's okay(ish).

You simply realize that life has
been prying your fingers from the
steering wheel for some time now.
And as you let go, you realize

the steering wheel was
never attached to anything
in the first place.

Sometimes
I fall into trust
842 times a day,

which is mostly because
I don't trust
anything

in between all the times
that I do.

"It's dark out there,"
you say, "I can't see
anything."

That is because you are
looking beyond the
edges of your own light.

How many times you forget:
looking forward into
the light you have

is always enough to take
the very next step.

You didn't ask to be a mosaic.

You didn't ask for all the shards
of who you were to be rearranged.

And each time life came and
shattered you, you tried *so* hard to
hold all the sharp pieces together.

You didn't know that life cracked
you in such a way that it harvested
the pieces it needed to make the
beautiful, light-catching mosaic
you are in the process of being,

and you missed the fact
that it simultaneously
whisked away all the pieces
that are not *you.*

"Everything is
falling
into place,"

I tell myself,
when everything is
falling.
[Unsure about the
"place" part.]

But then again,
the less I'm sure,
the less I'm in the way.

I step back and watch all the
falling
into all the places.

Made in the USA
Columbia, SC
24 November 2021

49735525R00024